Let's Learn About...
ENERGY

Written by Gordon Volke

TOPTHAT! Kids™

Copyright © 2004 Top That! Publishing plc
Top That! Publishing, 27023 McBean Parkway,
408 Valencia, CA 91355
Top That! is a Registered Trademark of
Top That! Publishing plc
www.topthatpublishing.com

Getting Started

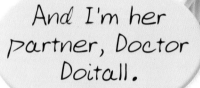

Hi! I'm Professor Tester.

And I'm her partner, Doctor Doitall.

We're keen young scientists. We love finding out things by doing experiments. Do you? That's cool! This book is full of fun things we can do together to find out more about ENERGY!

What Is Energy?

Energy is what makes something happen, whether it be moving or changing. You cannot see energy itself—you can only see what it does! There are many different types of energy and this book will tell you all about them.

What's In The Kit?

Inside your kit you will find everything you need to build a boat, a waterwheel and a rubber band-powered car. You'll be able to find lots of things around the house for the other experiments. Ask an adult to help you gather materials and equipment such as newspaper, scissors, a jug, pen or pencil and some string.

Colors of components may vary to those shown.

Let's Play Safe!

All the experiments in this book are safe to do, but make sure you stick to the rules.

PLEASE DO

✓ Always have an adult with you or nearby when you are doing an experiment. (The Golden Rule!)

✓ Clear up after your experiment and put back anything you have used or borrowed.

✓ Do the experiment properly. It is dangerous to mess about or be silly.

✓ Be patient! Experiments do not always work properly the first time.

PLEASE DON'T

❌ Handle anything sharp or use anything that is likely to break.

❌ Eat or drink anything when you are doing your experiment.

❌ Let your cat, dog or any other pets near your experiment. They could spoil it or get hurt themselves.

❌ Use anything that is not in your Fun Kit or on the list of things needed for your experiment.

❌ Try anything on your own. Always have an adult with you or nearby when you are doing any experiment.

Get A Move On!

The energy that makes something move is called kinetic energy.

The Car's A Star!

You can see kinetic energy at work by building this exciting model car powered by a rubber band.

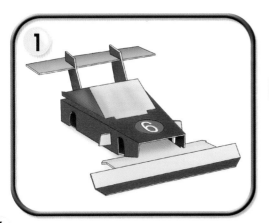

1 First slot together all the main body parts of the car, as shown in the picture.

2 Push one of the large wheels onto the end of one of the axles.

3 Now ask an adult to attach a piece of string to the end of your rubber band and push it through the wheel end of the axle. Remove the string.

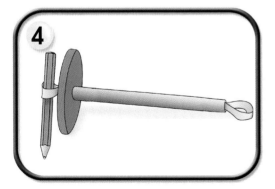

4 Push a small pencil through the end of your rubber band to stop it from going right through the axle.

5 Tape down the rubber band at the other end of the axle, then slide the axle through the holes at the back of the car. Slot on the other big wheel.

6 Push the other axle through the holes in the front of the car and slide on the two small wheels.

Now just wind the pencil round a few times and let go. The wheels will turn round and move the car.

Band Aid

It's the rubber band that provides the kinetic energy for your car. When the stretchy rubber is wound up tightly, energy builds up in the coils. When you let go, that energy is released.

And if it's connected to the wheels, the energy makes the wheels turn and... presto! Your car moves forward!

Make your own tests! See how far the car goes, how fast it goes and what happens when you wind that rubber band even tighter!

Let The Sunshine In

Energy from the sun is called solar energy. We need solar energy to make things grow.

Flower Power

Try this experiment to show the importance of sunshine in making things grow…

You will need:
- three small plants or flowers in flowerpots
- three saucers to go underneath
- two brown paper bags
- a watering can
- scissors

What You Do

Place the three plants in a sunny place, like on a windowsill, and water them all with the same amount of water.

1 Leave the first plant as it is.
2 Place a whole brown paper bag over the second one.
3 Ask a grown-up to cut a wide slit in the other paper bag and place it over the third plant.

Wait for about a week and then remove the covers.

What Do You Find?

Let The Sunshine In

Bright Is Right!

Your experiment should show the following results...

1 The plant that had no cover looks the best. It has had plenty of sunshine and has grown bigger and stronger.

2 The plant that was completely covered looks poor. It has had no sunshine and has not grown at all.

3 The plant covered by the bag with a slit in the side has grown towards the slit. It was searching for the few rays of sunshine that came in through the small hole.

So You Have Shown...

Solar energy, in the form of sunlight, affects how everything grows. The sun also influences rain and wind which are other sources of energy.

Turn, Turn, Turn!

Energy can be provided by water power.

What A Waterwheel!

You can catch the energy in flowing water by building this super working waterwheel.

You will need:
(all found in the kit)

- the slot-together waterwheel parts
- a plastic rod for the axle

1 Press out all of the waterwheel pieces before you begin.

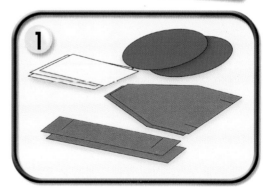

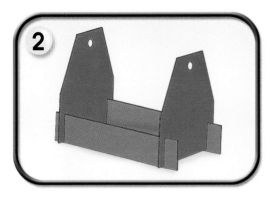

2 Start by building the stand. Do this by slotting together all of the red pieces, as shown.

3 Next slot the ends of the yellow pieces into the slits in the two blue discs.

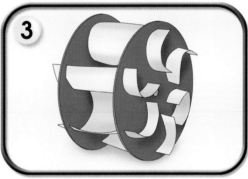

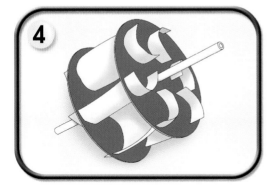

4 Push the plastic rod through the holes in the center of the discs.

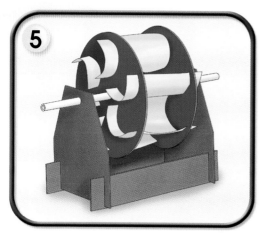

5 Now push the rod through the holes at each end of the stand.

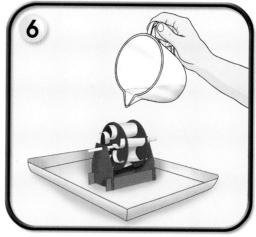

6 Place your waterwheel in a tray and pour on water. See how the wheel spins around.

Go With The Flow

When your waterwheel is put in a stream of running water, the energy in the water pushes the blades forward and this makes the wheel turn round.

So You Have Shown...

There is lots of energy in flowing water and it can be turned into movement.

Did You Know?
Giant water wheels like these use the energy in fast-flowing water to make electricity. This is called hydroelectric power.

Blowin' In The Wind

Energy can be provided by wind power.

Speed Super Boat!

You can feel the energy in the wind by experimenting with a simple toy boat. You'll find everything you need to make the boat in the kit.

You will need:

- hull of the boat from your kit
- plastic rod for the mast from your kit
- sail from your kit
- sticky putty from your kit
- a large bowl filled with water

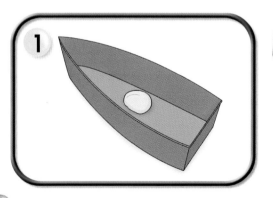

1

1 Stick a piece of sticky putty into the middle of the boat hull.

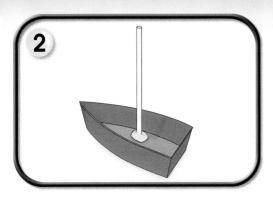

2 Push your plastic rod into the sticky putty. This will be the mast for your sail.

3 Now fit the sail onto the mast by pushing the mast between the two holes in the sail, as shown in the picture.

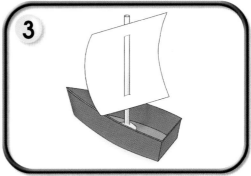

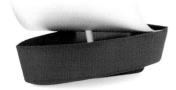

Time To Test Your Boat!

Put some water in a sink, in the bath or in a large container. Then place your boat on the water and blow on the sails. Watch it speed forward!

The energy contained in the wind is being caught by the sail and turned into forward movement.
The harder you blow, the more energy is provided and the faster your boat will travel.

So You Have Shown...

Wind power is a very strong and useful form of energy.

DO try this at home:

1 Count how long it takes your boat to travel the length of your container.

2 Blow harder and see how much quicker it travels.

3 See what happens when you make the water choppy.

4 Observe what happens if you fit a bigger sail.

5 Try fanning your boat with a magazine to make a really strong wind!

Whizzing Windmill

You can also feel the energy of the wind by building this cool hand-held windmill.

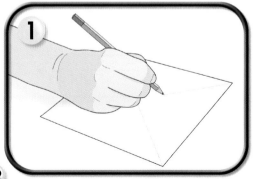

1 Draw straight lines on the paper or card, joining the four corners.

22

2 Ask an adult to make pinholes just beside the line in all four corners.

3 Cut along each line from the corner, stopping about half way to the center.

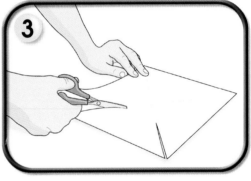

4 Fold each corner back to the center. The pinholes should all line up on top of one another.

5 Now ask an adult to push the pin through the pinholes and the center of the card. It should go into the eraser top of your pencil. Your windmill should be able to spin freely round and round.

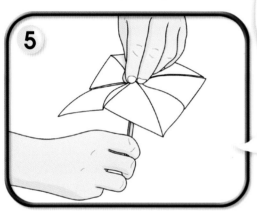

6 Your windmill is now finished. Blow on it and watch it go whizzing round.

Just as the sail of your boat picked up the energy in the air and turned it into forward movement, your windmill does the same and makes itself spin round and round.

Did You Know?

Windmills were first invented in the Middle East. It is thought that knights returning from the Crusades took the idea to Europe in the Middle Ages.

Modern windmills are connected to machines that make electricity from the power of the wind.

Wind Energy

A windmill's sails use the energy from the wind to turn machinery which grinds corn to flour.

Hubble, Bubble!

The world of chemical energy is exciting! Try this experiment to see the energy released when certain chemicals are mixed together.

You will need:
- baking soda
- malt vinegar
- a clean, empty jar
- a teaspoon

1 Put two or three teaspoonfuls of baking soda into the jar.

2 Now pour a little vinegar onto the baking soda.

Energy from the mixture of baking soda and vinegar is released in the form of frothing bubbles and also a little heat. So see if your jar feels a little bit warm after the experiment.

So You Have Shown...
Strong bursts of energy are produced when certain chemicals are mixed together.

 Warning... Warning...Warning!
Don't try mixing any other chemicals on your own. It is very dangerous and could injure you or make you ill.

Good Vibrations

Energy can also come in the form of sound waves and vibrations.

This trick is quick, easy and brilliant fun. Demonstrate how sound vibrations need energy to travel through the air!

1 Hold the watch by your ear to hear it ticking. Move it away until you cannot hear it anymore. Take a note of how far you have to move it before you cannot hear its ticking.

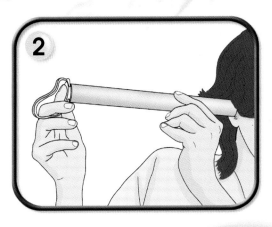

2 Hold the tube to your ear and hold the watch to the other end. Notice how you can hear the watch ticking much more clearly than without the tube.

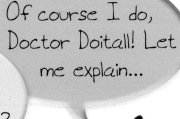

Of course I do, Doctor Doitall! Let me explain...

Do you know how this works, Professor Tester?

So You Have Shown...

Sound vibrations require energy to travel over a distance. When they start traveling they spread out and lose energy.

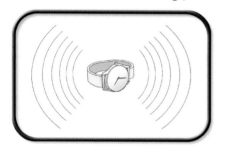

When the tube is there, however, these sound vibrations do not spread out as much and therefore lose less energy as they travel.

Did you know?

Musical instruments with strings, like the guitar and violin, work in just the same way. The strings vibrate when they are plucked or strummed, sending out waves of sound energy. These travel through the air and are heard as music when they reach our ears.

All Fall Down

Gravity is a type of energy that we feel all the time. It is the force that pulls us downward, making everything fall to the ground. Without the pull of gravity, we would all float away!

You will need:
- an old book
- a metal coin
- a piece of paper
- a feather

Just Drop It, Will You?

Try this experiment to show how gravity works and how different objects are affected by it.

Warning... Warning!
You MUST have an adult with you if you climb up anywhere high.

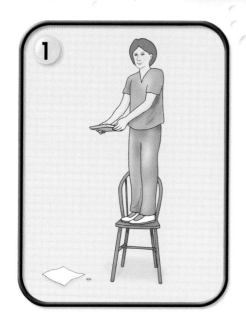

2 Drop the objects, one by one, and watch how they fall to the ground.

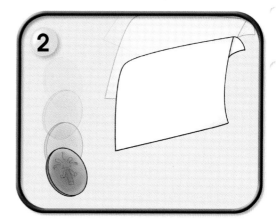

1 Stand on a chair or climb the stairs—somewhere to gain some height.

3 Work out which object falls the fastest and which falls the slowest.

So You Have Shown...

All four objects fall, so gravity pulls down on everything. The book and the coin fall faster than the piece of paper and the feather. Very light objects, like the paper and the feather, are so light that the air holds them up, working against the force of gravity.

Swinging The Bucket!

Try this experiment to show how gravity works and how objects are affected by it.

You will need:
- a bucket
- water

⚠ Warning...Warning!
Remember to make sure that everyone watching is well out of the way before you start swinging.

1 Half fill a plastic bucket with water. Stand outside and swing it in a circle.

2 If you swing the bucket round fast enough, no water will spill out of it!

So You Have Shown...

When you swing the bucket round, you force it to change direction. However, the water inside the bucket tries to travel in straight lines. The water is pushed against the inside of the bucket and cannot escape!

Did You Know?

The force of gravity was first discovered about 400 years ago by a brilliant young scientist called Sir Isaac Newton. It is said (though it may not be true) that Newton realized a force was at work when an apple dropped beside him in the orchard where he was reading.

The pull of gravity is the strongest on Earth. On the Moon, there is only a little bit, so astronauts can get around by taking huge "moon jumps." In the spaceship and in outer space, there is no gravity at all, so people and objects float around as if they're in water!

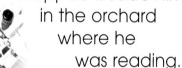

The Flick Of A Switch

The lights and heating in your house, your TV, radio and computer are all powered by electrical energy.

Static Electricity

This trick makes something amazing happen by using electric charge, or static electricity.

You will need:
- a plastic pen
- small pieces of tissue paper
- a cloth

1 Charge up a plastic pen with static electricity by rubbing it vigorously with a cloth.

2 Hold the charged pen over the small pieces of tissue paper, and watch as the paper appears to dance.

So You Have Shown...

A pen is charged with static electricity when you rub it.
And the static electricity attracts the tissue paper.

Did You Know?

The electricity we use every day comes from different sources…

Old King Coal

When coal is burned in big amounts, the heat and light it creates can be turned into lots of electricity. This is still the main source of electric power.

Oil Do The Job

Oil is very similar to coal, except that it is a runny liquid rather than hard stone. When burned, it also makes electricity and powers our cars.

Hey! Not So Fast!

Coal and oil are known as fossil fuels. They are running out very fast and will soon be used up. So the world could run short of electrical energy.

Falling Out About Nuclear Power

Huge amounts of electricity can also be made cheaply in nuclear power plants. Some people say this is a good thing. Other people say it is dangerous. Nobody is sure which is right.

So what's the answer to our power problem? We must find new ways to make electrical energy… and we must save the electricity we do have!

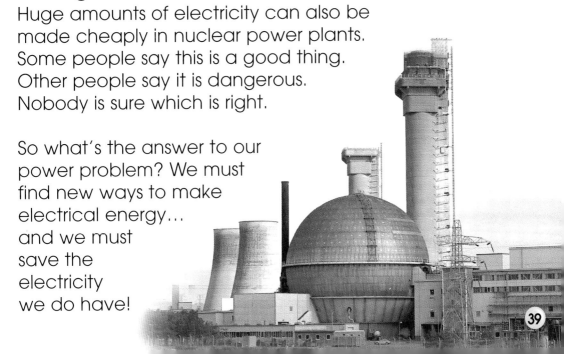

Don't Use it... Or Lose It!

If we can all save heat, light and water and use things again instead of throwing them away, the world's energy supplies will not run out so fast.

You will need:
- four clean, empty jars
- one cotton sock
- one woolen sock
- a large piece of paper
- tinfoil
- a thermometer
- a tray
- a large jug

Why You Insulate!

This experiment shows you which materials are best at stopping heat escaping.

1 Put the jars onto the tray and ask an adult to fill them with hot water.
(Not too hot or there's a danger of being scalded!)

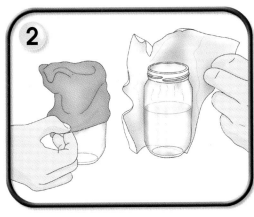

2 Carefully put the socks over two of the jars whilst the adult wraps the other two, one in paper and the other in tinfoil.

3 Leave the tray outside in the cold for about 15-20 minutes. Then take the temperatures of each jar with the thermometer.

Which one has stayed the hottest? Which is now the coldest?

Different materials keep heat in better than others. You should find that the jars covered in tinfoil and the woolen sock were the warmest. The jars covered in paper and the cotton should have lost their heat more quickly.

So You Have Shown...

Tinfoil and wool keep the heat in and can be called good insulators.

This Is Rubbish!

Another way to save energy is by recycling. This means using objects again rather than throwing them away. Then they won't be wasted.

Have You Got The Bottle?

Here's a fun way to recycle old glass bottles. Use them to make a bottle orchestra!

You will need:
- four glass bottles, clean and empty
- food colorings
- water
- a stick

1 Put your bottles in a straight line and fill them with different amounts of water, starting with the least and adding a little more each time.

2 Ask an adult to add some food coloring to make the water in the bottles into different colors.

3 Hit the bottles gently with the stick. You'll find they make different sounds.

What tune can you play?

What's For Tea Tonight?

We get energy from food! Eating food is what gives you the strength to run and play.

Mr Smiley Banana Face

Try this recipe for a tasty treat. It contains bananas which are full of healthy food energy.

You will need:
- one or two ripe bananas
- tin or pot of ready-made custard
- glacé cherries
- a small dish

1 Ask a grown-up to peel the banana and cut it into bite-size pieces.

2 Put the banana slices into the serving dish and pour the custard all over them.

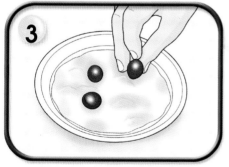

3 Finally, make a face on the banana custard by adding banana slices and cherries.

Bananas give you energy because they contain natural sugar. This is also found in other fruits such as apples, pears and oranges. You should eat plenty of fruit to stay healthy. Sugar from candies, cakes and cookies is not good for you. You should always try to eat food that's good for you.

We have to go now. It's tea time.

This food will keep up our energy levels. Then we can keep learning about energy! GOODBYE!